Jimmy Hoffa: The Controversial Life and Disapp᷍᷍᷍ ᷍᷍ ᷍᷍ ᷍ Godfather of the Teamsters

By Charles River Editors

About Charles River Editors

Charles River Editors provides superior editing and original writing services across the digital publishing industry, with the expertise to create digital content for publishers across a vast range of subject matter. In addition to providing original digital content for third party publishers, we also republish civilization's greatest literary works, bringing them to new generations of readers via ebooks.

Sign up here to receive updates about free books as we publish them, and visit Our Kindle Author Page to browse today's free promotions and our most recently published Kindle titles.

Introduction

Hoffa and Bernard Spindel in 1957

Jimmy Hoffa (1913-disappeared 1975)

"I've told you before and I'll tell you again. The strong survive and the weak disappear. We do not intend to disappear." - Jimmy Hoffa

"'He's not just the most powerful man in labor,' Robert Kennedy had said in the wake of Hoffa's announcement; 'he's the most powerful man in the country, next to the President.'" – Arthur A. Sloane, *Hoffa*

A century ago, if one were to come across a manual laborer from the early 20th century or the Roaring Twenties and relayed to them the possibility of one day sticking it to The Man, one would probably be laughed out of the century. However, this was exactly what one man with solid-gold aspirations and audacity set out to achieve. Jimmy Hoffa, once described by Bobby Kennedy as the second most powerful man in America, was a union boss who evoked both respect and fear, and he continues to be a legendary figure who often crops up in conversation and media over 40 years after his disappearance. While it was an open secret that Hoffa had shady connections, the success of his leadership allowed supporters to overlook them. As Sloane put it, "More apparent to Teamster members than any moral lapses were the tangible gains that had been steadily realized under Hoffa since his advent to power."

Charles Brandt once wrote, "From 1955 until 1965 Jimmy Hoffa was as famous as Elvis Presley. From 1965 until 1975 Jimmy Hoffa was as famous as the Beatles." But as famous as he was in life, it was Jimmy Hoffa's demise that continues to fascinate the country. On July 30, 1975, Hoffa drove to an important meeting at the Machus Red Fox Restaurant, but he was never seen or heard from again. To this day, authorities are still searching for him (or presumably his remains), having been overloaded with false and dead-end leads throughout the decades. By championing the hearts and loyalty of America's trucking industry and arousing fear in the public for his rumored mob connections, earning a couple of enemies along the way was inevitable for Hoffa, but the mystery remains. Naturally, people have put forward ridiculous theories to explain his disappearance, but either way, it's fair to say that the legendary life and times of the controversial and still-missing Teamster leader have produced one of the world's most baffling ongoing mysteries for good reason.

Jimmy Hoffa: The Controversial Life and Disappearance of the Godfather of the Teamsters chronicles the tumultuous life of Jimmy Hoffa, one oozing with action and glory but also full of sinister entanglements with the criminal underworld. The book also looks at the enigma of his life and disappearance, exploring the most credible, fascinating, and downright nutty theories surrounding his persistently debated fate. Along with pictures and a bibliography, you'll learn about Hoffa like never before.

Jimmy Hoffa: The Controversial Life and Disappearance of the Godfather of the Teamsters

About Charles River Editors

Introduction

Chapter 1: Hard Knocks

Chapter 2: Putting a Foot Down

Chapter 3: The Kennedys

Chapter 4: Shame, Shackles, and a Stab in the Back

Chapter 5: Clinging Onto the Glory Days

Chapter 6: Theories

Online Resources

Bibliography

Chapter 1: Hard Knocks

"I do to others what they do to me, only worse." - Hoffa

A beam of dawn sunlight skims across your drowsy eyes, coaxing you to lucidity. You rub at your squinched vision with calloused and blistered fingers, a half-inch stub where your pinkie used to be. Swallowing a chunk of stale, flavorless bread that barely appeases your rumbling stomach, you proceed to mechanically slip into your grimy overalls and head straight to work. Approaching the gloomy collection of factory buildings, you remember how you used to wrap a pulled sleeve around your face to guard you from the eerily black smog pouring out of chimneys and cheap machinery. Now, you simply trudge in through the doors unfazed, the pollution the least of your problems. Taking position behind your station, you pick up from where you left off yesterday, latching onto the controls of the enormous punch press equipment. You have an undeniable love-hate relationship with the selfsame machine riddled with safety hazards, but has also kept you afloat on the dinghy of poverty for years. The sticky, stifling heat enveloping you in an unwelcome embrace, you wipe the sweat off your brows and carry on with the tedious task of stamping steel splices for street poles. Your eyes are deliberately riveted to your assignment, careful not to catch a glimpse at the dusty clock fixed on the wall. Roughly three minutes in, it's just another 10 hours and 57 minutes before you get to punch out. Still, you're grateful you're fortunate enough to be employed, what with your three tykes to feed back home. The six dollars waiting for you at the end of the week could make or break all of you. Hoffa himself once said of his childhood meals, "A slab of bread buttered with lard, and if you were lucky, seasoned with salt and pepper. That was a luxury."

Workplace conditions for the average working man at the start of the 20th century were, needless to say, less than deplorable, and that scenario can readily be contrasted to that of Simon Dempsey, who in 2011 went through the effort of filing 10 "formal" complaints after suffering outrages that included having his lunchbox infiltrated and the sandwich replaced with a pickle. In Simon's eyes, these offenses warranted immediate "disciplinary action." Nowadays, taking for granted the comfortable temperature set on the office thermostat, sneaking onto social media on company time, and blasting the boss for refusing to allot an extra 20 minutes into hour-long lunch breaks aren't all that unheard of, and today it can be difficult to imagine that serious offenses such as bullying or sexual harassment had to take place before workplace etiquette rules were established. In fact, corporations and fellow "big guys" have now become the ones scrutinized on slides, stumbling over themselves to keep their image as squeaky-clean as possible.

In the 21st century, when people study the vintage, grainy portraits of candid faces and stiffly posed subjects in sepia and monochrome tones produced by 20th century photographs, most are naturally drawn to the dramatic difference in their lives. But beyond the whimsy of full-bodied swimming costumes, young ladies' ornate, wide-brimmed hats, and lunching immigrants perched upon a beam suspended over the city view, knowing that half of all children nationwide were living in poverty probably sours the grape. The average family was too busy scrounging to get by for luxuries such as telephones, cars, and indoor plumbing, with working families raking in a measly $3,000 a year in the 1910s, and back then, the blatant abuse of power displayed by corporations and the wealthy class was verging on ludicrous. Though a few labor unions existed throughout the country, with the National Labor Union in place since the mid-19th century, it appeared as if little actual change was taking effect.

The snail-paced progress and looming threat of poverty weighing over their heads took its toll on depressed millions, but for one man, this was merely a challenge he was eager to get his hands on. Born James Riddle Hoffa on the 14th of February in 1913, to say that his unique middle name foreshadowed his fate is as cheesy as it is accurate. The Hoffas resided in the small, charming city of Brazil, Indiana with a population of less than 10,000, so small that the inhabitants would be capable of roaming freely through Michigan Stadium, which houses 10 times that number of patrons. Jimmy was the third of four children born to a Pennsylvania Dutch coal miner named John Hoffa and an Irish immigrant named Viola Riddle. His mother would prove to be equally industrious, taking care of laundry for neighboring families and taking up odd jobs to contribute to the household.

Together, the Hoffas settled in a modest one-story house topped with a tiny attic, as plain as the next house in the neighborhood. The area was known as "Stringtown," popularized for the community's abundance of low-class coal miner households. Thus, it is little surprise that young Jimmy was well-acquainted with hardship and financial strife from the womb, and his parents – especially John – keeping him well-rounded with the harsh cruelty of the real world. Some would say he was forced to mature at a young age, and though he was deprived of spinning tops, rocking horses, and fancy push-and-pull toys that were all the rage those days, Jimmy adored his parents. In particular, he shared an exceptional bond with his hardworking father, who taught his son a valuable life lesson about the importance of honest, hard work and its impending success, qualities he idolized and aspired to as he grew older.

However, when Jimmy turned 7, a sudden, preventable loss would leave a permanent scarring in his abruptly upturned world. His father and primary role model died as a result of a horrid disease accumulated in the coal factories of his employer, an independent prospector: black lung. The name of the deteriorating disease is quite literal, as it destroyed the rosy-pink organ from the inside out, and some of the worst cases of blackened lungs uncovered during autopsies were found crusted over with a coarse, nightmarishly black shell, almost as it were transforming into a lump of coal itself. When people inhaled clouds of coal mine dust and toxic fumes from faulty machinery, they were taking a chance with their life, and that's even before mentioning the need to dodge falling boulders and potentially undetectable gas explosions. Due to the ignorance and dreadful lack of care demonstrated by such employers, it was only a matter of time before some workers became statistics in what was a shocking but all too legal death trap.

Even at his fragile, impressionable age, Jimmy understood his father's death was a direct result of his tragically substandard working conditions. After John's untimely passing, Viola did her best to keep their heads above water. Around this time, the 19th Amendment had only just been approved to grant women the right to vote, but since she was unimpressively educated and not a man, employers weren't in a rush to hire her. Nonetheless, with four starving mouths to feed, she powered through, her maternal instincts on turbo-charge.

In 1924, when Jimmy was 11, the family packed up and headed up north to Detroit. Viola found work at a local laundry, and after her mundane shifts, she picked up extra work polishing radiator caps at an auto-parts factory. But even as the poor mother worked day and night juggling two jobs while raising four kids, making ends meet was still a battle. Both Jimmy and his older brother Billy were spurred on by their parents' inherent determination; to help out with the family's financial conundrums, they began shining shoes and delivering clean clothes to their mother's customers.

By the age of 12, Jimmy took it upon himself to take up a weekend job bagging potatoes at a neighborhood grocery store. These days, many millennials gripe about "boredom" as they lounge on their beds and voyage the world through the tips of their fingers. Instead of tearing one's eyes away from *Netflix* queues and intrusive celebrity gossip, a growing sense of entitlement seems to bar humanity from venturing out the comforts of their rooms for some old-fashioned menial labor. In fact, many choose to tend to virtual farms and establishments with the kind of diligence to a non-existent boss behind a screen a real-life employer could only dream of. Back in the day, however, education was a special prerogative saved for mostly the higher class, with scores of children dropping out from school to work in hard labor. Jimmy was no different.

An interesting aspect about his character was that he could have suffered from Napoleon complex, having always been something of a runt amongst his peers, as noted by authorities in the *Biography Channel* episode "Jimmy Hoffa: The Man behind the Mystery." This was further backed by an interview with his daughter Barbara, who shared one of her father's favorite childhood memories with the audience. As the story goes, on one of the boys' deliveries, they were approached by a couple of hoodlums who outnumbered the brothers, roughing them up and causing the clothes to tumble out of their basket. Angered by the fact that his mother would now have to redo the washing, Jimmy simply "took care of them," after which the brothers were never bothered again. Later, when Jimmy tried to blend in with the city kids in Detroit, he was ostracized for being a "hillbilly." Even as he was taunted, the short adolescent – perhaps also fueled by the rage that comes with puberty – fought off his Goliaths. There was a fearless fire in Jimmy that sparked even as a child, never needing to think twice to stand his ground.

In the 9th grade, at the age of 14, Jimmy left school to work full-time, having by now scaled the ranks to delivery boy. He continued working at the grocery store for two more years, and when the stock market crashed in 1929, he found employment unloading produce at Kroger Grocery

Company. Still one of the nation's leading supermarket chains to this day, little did anyone know that this branch in Detroit would truly mark the inception of Hoffa's coming career, and ultimately, his legacy.

Chapter 2: Putting a Foot Down

"Nobody in this country respects what's weak. You believe me! If you see a beggar on a corner, with his hat in his hand, nobody respects him. Dress the same man up, give him an air of dignity, and he can command respect. The same thing applies to this union." – Jimmy Hoffa

With America just at the onset of the decade-long economic spiral, a morose uneasiness gripped the nation's civilians, and the competition for employment was as heated as ever. The job pool had become even shallower, with over 1,550,000 unemployed the year of the stock market crash, and this number sadly only multiplied as the years dragged on in the Depression. The worst of the era arrived in 1933, when the country saw 12,830,000 Americans without any means of income.

Understandably, the jobless were becoming desperate, and people's will to survive got the better of many. The dreary times saw countless citizens resort to thievery and violence to keep their families alive, while those who were blessed enough to still have jobs had no choice but to keep their mouths shut when the bigwigs decided to reduce their wages, hours, and workforce, hoping they wouldn't be the next ones under the ax. All the while, most were finding it increasingly difficult to tighten their belts, down to the last hole on their straps.

Not surprisingly, during this time the executives at Kroger Grocery found it in their best interests to exploit their faltering staff. Jimmy, along with his fellow coworkers, were only being paid when they were in the actual act of unloading goods and produce, meaning the employees weren't being compensated for the rest of the day while they stood around waiting for the next cargo truck to steer through the warehouse doors. Unfortunately, Kroger was hardly alone when it came to this, as almost every huge corporation in America acted the same way. At this point, unskilled laborers were only raking in an average of 36 cents an hour, roughly the equivalent of $4.56 today, and as a result, morale among the staff was at its lowest juncture. Jimmy watched day in and day out as his somber coworkers grudgingly trudged in and out the doors broke and miserable, with their job security all but nonexistent. Frames of once proud men were slackened in defeat, but at the same time, everyone seemed to constantly be on edge, looking to take the lights out of anyone who even slightly threatened their job.

Dave Johnson, whose company once hauled for *Kroger,* remembered young Jimmy fondly and later asserted that the young teen made a lasting impression on him even from their first meeting. He would interact with Jimmy, who sometimes unloaded his truck, and he described Hoffa as a "tough guy" with a mean mug. Though it was obvious the teenager despised his job, he was one of the hardest workers Johnson had ever come across, and he earned the respect of his coworkers, most of whom were much older than he was. Everyone else was seemingly resigned to their fates, but not Jimmy; if anything, when injustice appeared, his resolution only became more unyielding.

Fittingly, the teenager was the one of the first to join the local union that formed in the area. At this time, the union was virtually empty, with only a handful of members occupying a single sign-up sheet. Knowing that they were expendable, most weren't looking to jeopardize their jobs, especially in the midst of the tumultuous economy, but that wasn't the case with Hoffa. Still incensed by his father's death, who was taken just shy of his 40th birthday and left the family with no benefits or financial security, Jimmy thirsted for change.

In February 1931, the young man had entered legal adulthood, but not an iota of improvement had taken effect in his workplace. Hours were just as long and wages just as low, and reports of drivers falling asleep behind the wheel from exhaustion were rocketing. A few months later, as Jimmy and his coworkers were unloading crates of strawberries from the back of a truck, the 18 year-old decided to take action. Backed by a coworker named Robert "Bobby" Holmes, a former coal miner, Jimmy upturned a crate, heightening himself amongst his peers in the center of the loading dock. Clearing his throat, he called out to his fellow coworkers. His eyes glittering with conviction, he lifted a hand boldly in the air and called out for a complete work stoppage. Holmes recalled how the small man swelled up with pride, unflinching at the 175 warehouse workers blinking back at him. Listing each and every unfair work grievance they were forced to endure, he declared that they would endure them no more. Slowly but surely, his coworkers became equally enraged, agreeing that they would halt their tasks until their needs were met.

The bargaining chips set in place were the several hundred boxes of fresh strawberries in the closed quarters, exposed to the muggy spring heat. The strawberries needed to be iced immediately to prevent spoilage, and with the company's business already on turbulent waters, they couldn't afford the loss of such a large order. The Kroger night manager ultimately stepped into the rowdy warehouse, teeming with burly workers pumped up on adrenaline and fury, and as he edged past the glaring workers, Jimmy handed him a detailed list of the workers' complaints. The manager later agreed to arrange a meeting with management the following day if the workers continued their work. Satisfied and feeling victorious, Jimmy and his coworkers, who dubbed themselves the "Strawberry Boys," gladly resumed the taxing task of unloading crates, anxious for the next day to come.

Headed by Jimmy, the Strawberry Boys arrived promptly the next day for their meeting with Kroger management, starting a basic back-and-forth negotiation that stretched for a few days. Hoffa would later explain his bargaining philosophy: "There is a time to be tough, a time to be adamant, a time to be open to compromise, and a time to reach agreement." The employees emerged triumphant in the end with a new one-page contract, which included solidifying their work hours and guaranteeing each worker a 13 cent raise per hour. Impressed with what the spunky teenager had managed to achieve, Sam Calhoun, a 39-year-old radical and former employee of the Railway Express Agency, appointed him Vice-President of his one-company union. Jimmy's coworker, Holmes, was made secretary-treasurer.

Jimmy knew he had finally found his calling, but the victory proved to be short-lived. The next year, Kroger refused to renew the contract initially agreed on, and both Jimmy and Holmes were yanked from their position in the company union and local charter. However, even as it appeared as if they were right back where they'd started, Jimmy ultimately refused to let this turn of events hold him back.

One of Hoffa's most significant relationships would come at this stage in his life. As he neared his 20s, he started a "love affair" with a young woman by the name of Sylvia Pagano, a sultry beauty with a clerical job at the labor union. Though both had gone their separate ways by 1934, with Sylvia moving to Kansas City to marry a driver named Frank O'Brien (legally changed from Sam Scaradino), they still kept in touch. Frank Coppola, one of the most dangerous mobsters in Detroit at the time, was made godfather of O'Brien's baby boy, and when Frank died, Coppola began a relationship with Sylvia. Through the young widow, Hoffa was introduced to Coppola, and it was through this connection that the young adult dipped his toe into the deep, deep pool of the city's criminal underworld.

Coppola

By 1935, different union factions had begun forming, and it looked like the movement was gaining traction in Detroit. On the second floor of a massive brick building on Trumbull Avenue and Fort Street were several union headquarters, including the Locals 674 (fish peddlers), 247 (coal loaders), 285 (laundry drivers), and 299 (general freight.) Banded together, they were known as the Detroit Teamsters Joint Council 43. A year later, a man by the name of R.J. Bennett, the secretary-treasurer of Local 247 coal loaders, took over for the Local 299, and together with Sam Hurst, president of the Joint Council, they merged membership of the fish peddlers into 299.

By this time, Jimmy was 22 and disgruntled, and he began to act up even more frequently at the docking platforms. His brazen words and tendency to speak his mind often incited furious, thronging mobs that regularly disrupted work at Kroger, but even when he was eventually fired, he was scooped up by Bennett, who admired his feisty zest for justice. Jimmy was awarded the full-time job of union organizer for the Joint Council, where he began working directly with the hauling drivers of Local 299.

Upon entering the Local 299 unit, Jimmy took in the dilapidated, almost pathetic surroundings, and given its small membership of only 250, he knew he had to breathe new life into the unit and its members. As he carried on with his new responsibilities, the heads of the unions were thoroughly awed at his strong work ethic, which stood out distinctly from the desolate masses beaten down by the cruel days of the Great Depression. Largely influenced by the opinionated organizer with an affinity for raising morale, the membership soared to over 4,000 Teamsters. When a union member was asked what it was about Jimmy that seemed to magnetize people by the flock, they explained Jimmy's relatable, down-to-earth-disposition. Jimmy knew everyone by name and made certain to make eye contact with everyone he interacted with, while never giving a limp handshake. They admired his tenacity and his willingness to brave the conditions front and center at picket lines and during strikes, his voice always the loudest amongst the sea of protesters.

When 1936 came along, Jimmy's name was well known in the community. That March, he was approached by a group of female laundry workers who had caught wind of his influence and troubled him for advice on organizing their own strike. His enraptured gaze landed on the delicate features of a 17-year-old Polish woman named Josephine, and in his own words, he felt like he'd been "hit in the chest by a blackjack." Instantly smitten with each other and acting on the connection both felt and openly admitted to, they began a brief period of wooing and sweet courtship, enjoying each other's company on several dates. Acting spontaneously on the unique chemistry they shared, they had a simple marriage in the fall at the Justice of the Peace, and later that year, they purchased a small home in Robson Drive, their first home and Jimmy's pride and joy.

It has been said that Jimmy's mother Viola often criticized their marriage. Along with disapproving of Josephine, she failed to get along with Jimmy's in-laws. Some believed this was because to the average outsider, it would appear as if Jimmy and Josephine were polar opposites. Josephine harbored a wild side, enjoying parties and cocktails when the opportunities presented themselves, whereas Jimmy, who seemed to have no vices, was the working-stiff type who went out of his way to avoid alcohol. However, despite their differences, the couple loved each other deeply and stuck faithfully by each other's side through thick and thin. Jimmy fondly nicknamed his wife the "Sargent" because she was the only one whose orders he would listen to, and later in life, they would have two children: Jimmy, Jr. and Barbara. In interviews, his children have insisted that even though Jimmy was hardly around, never once did they feel unloved. During the fleeting instances he had free time, he would take them on memorable fishing and hunting trips, always showing them his undying attention during the little time he had with them.

The Hoffa family

Hoffa and his son

By 1937, the war between the unions and the corporations was in disarray. Strikes and protests were proliferating by the minute, and when law enforcement had become insufficient and powerless against the hell-raising employees, they took matters into their own hands. Menacing mobsters selected from the criminal underbelly of Detroit were hired by management to brutally intimidate their employees into staying in line, but the hired thugs often attacked peaceful demonstrators unprovoked, leading to the unnecessary bloodshed. One of the worst instances took place in May of that year. During the infamous Republic Steel Massacre in Chicago on May 30th, 1937, over 100 workers and their families in the middle of a public demonstration were pelted with bullets by panicking police officers and hired black market help. To add to the controversy, most were found with bullets embedded in their backs as they fled, and as a result, the lives of 10 protesters and family members were lost that day. Prior to this, there had been the Ludlow Massacre, a notorious protest that took place two decades earlier and claimed the lives of at least 26 coal miners and their families. This included two women and 11 children, who asphyxiated and burned to death under one tent.

In spite of all the rising tension, R.J. Bennett was adamant that this was finally the year they would make progress against management. The Teamsters weren't progressing with the speed they had primarily intended, as wages were at a stand-still, prices of commodities were staunchly rising, and most importantly, the workers were getting restless. Authorized by the union, Bennett, along with Jimmy, who closely studied and learned his every move, called for the very first city-wide strike in April. Bennett claimed Jimmy as his shining star for the strikes amongst the Teamsters, which lasted for a total of three days. Prior to the protests, Teamsters were largely pacified by lackluster bribes of sorts to reimburse their scant wages, but receiving an occasional gift of turkey or ham during the holidays and syrupy, empty words followed by meaningless handshakes to compensate them for their long hours and backbreaking work just wasn't cutting it anymore. By the end of the strikes, city drivers were granted a rise of 60 cents per hour and cross-border drivers were pocketing $5 for each trip to Chicago.

Now in his mid-20s, Jimmy was only becoming more resourceful with his out-of-the-box thinking. Although he was now married to Josephine and remained entirely dedicated to her, he still maintained connections he had formed through Sylvia, and one of them was Santo Perrone, who by this time had become chief of "union busting." Perrone introduced him to Angelo Meli, a close acquaintance who headed a covert drop-off point that stored heavy weaponry, including rifles and machine guns, sent to the mob in Detroit from New York. The supposed reason the strikes had gone so smoothly was because Jimmy used his connections with Perrone and Meli, asking them to keep the mob at bay during the scuffle between union and management. Even though it looked as if Jimmy had formed an alliance with the mobsters, his acquaintances retained that he had merely figured out who was going to attack and cordially requested for them to back off. With the mobs a no-show, along with the Strawberry Boys, who by now had plenty of experience roughhousing under their belt, the Teamsters successfully fended off whatever muscle management was able to scrape up.

Perrone

Meli

Even with the progress, Local 299 had still not granted them the contract renewal from Kroger, so in the spring of 1937 the warehouse workers applied for their own charter. They became known as Local 337, and what would ensue would be a drawn-out, unruly conflict that would span over 18 months. It was during this battle that the Strawberry Boys would become renowned for their bravery fighting the power. On the other end, the law enforcement despised the union, thus backing the seemingly heartless corporations.

The Strawberry Boys and truckers held great pride in their defense tactics, and their violence on par with the management muscle. Most armed themselves with tire irons and other blunt objects for protection, while some brandished guns in the face of authority. As Calhoun and Martin Haggerty, one of Jimmy's cohorts who helped him organize the famous strawberry strike of '31, fought off a Kroger watchman, the latter was shot in the arm. Holmes was dragged off behind bars on multiple occasions, and Jimmy himself was beaten up a total of 24 times, requiring stitches to seal up wounds and gashes opened up by cops and management muscle.

Still, in spite of the serious violence targeted at him that resulted from the special attention management showered him with, Hoffa never shied away from a fight. Josephine supported this through the stories she'd tell their children, remembering how their father would come home with his shirt soaked through and dripping with blood and one side of his head gashed open. She would patch him up temporarily and plead with him to stay home, but he would just charge back out the doors, only to return home later with the other side of his head split.

At the same time, it would also soon become clear that people could not double-cross Jimmy without repercussions. When Jimmy was betrayed after aiding the Minneapolis Teamsters leader, Farrell Dobbs, in organizing the truckers under the Center States Drivers Council, he helped the federal government squash Dobbs' union. Though Jimmy was revered by his peers, he always showed a firm hand in toughness, enforcing it when the Detroit Teamsters' union felt imperiled. In 1941, Jimmy sought the help of the "East Side Crowd," a group of mobsters notorious for their brutal methods of handling business. The ESC effectively drove the rival union out of town.

Dobbs

Jimmy began climbing the ranks to power during the 1940s. First, he became Vice President of the Central States Drivers Council, and then President of the Michigan Conference of Teamsters. He was eventually appointed President of Joint Council 43 in Detroit. In 1952, he broke through the barriers of locality and landed himself the role of Vice President of the International Brotherhood of Teamsters (IBT) countrywide. A year later, Jimmy became President of the Central Conference of Teamsters, granting him the responsibility of chief negotiator in 20 states.

With his power and hold expanding at lightning speed, more and more union leaders called for him to help out with their strikes. With the bargaining methods Jimmy had rooted into the system, truckers would later win their first national contract in 1964.

At this stage in Jimmy's life, everything seemed to be going swimmingly and according to plan, but trouble was brewing close at hand.

Chapter 3: The Kennedys

"But to hear Kennedy when he was grandstanding in front of the McClellan Committee you might have thought I was making as much out of the pension fund as the Kennedys made out of selling whiskey." – Jimmy Hoffa

Right as the year 1957 kicked off, the U.S. Senate began a meticulous investigation of labor unions following allegations and reports of labor racketeering. Hearings graced every screen on television, and citizens tuned in to watch the hearings surrounding "improper activities" in the labor and management fields. The movement to scour through the details of labor and management activity was headed by Senator John McClellan, and over the course of two years, the McClellan Committee dug and dug.

McClellan

Eventually, they struck gold by unearthing a tangled tapestry of the Teamsters' under-the-radar corruption. In August of that year, Jimmy was hauled in as a witness for questioning at a televised hearing that would have the nation abuzz, starting his 7-year feud with Bobby Kennedy, brother of then Massachusetts Senator John F. Kennedy.

Bobby and Jimmy came from opposite ends of the spectrum. Whereas Jimmy came from very humble beginnings and failed to complete the 9th grade, Bobby was a Harvard graduate with the most white collar roots. Serving as Chief Counsel for the U.S. Senate Committee, the smartly dressed 32 year old sported a neatly-combed haircut covering a high forehead and had a desk of similarly attired suits. The Chief Counsel made it his primary cause to wipe out the organized crime he believed was corrupting honest labor unions, and he believed with every bone in his body that Jimmy Hoffa was one of the masterminds behind the corruption. Jimmy needed to be stopped, and Bobby felt he was the man to do it.

Bobby Kennedy

The Kennedy brothers working on the committee

Bobby stared down his smug opponent, ready to fire off a round of hard-hitting questions, but across the room, Hoffa, 12 years his senior, sat firm and stony-faced, ready to deflect each question his rival had in store for him. Though the fully grown man was only 5'5", thanks to his stocky physique, coupled with intense features set upon a sturdy, squared jaw, Jimmy appeared and acted as if he were twice his size. He gazed back with his beady, grayish-blue eyes narrowed, the slightest bit of intimidation absent in his impenetrable, unabashed demeanor.

Bobby asked question after question about Jimmy's boss, David Beck, then-president of the IBT, but he had no courtroom experience and was described by spectators as being unprofessional, with many believing Jimmy had gotten the better of him. It would seem that Jimmy would anticipate the next question even before he was interrogated, skating past his questions with slippery, well-worded answers. The nation watched as Jimmy further antagonized Bobby throughout the length of the hearing, winking and catching the counsel off guard, fruitfully delaying and dismantling their trains of thought.

The only time Jimmy seemed to lose his cool was when Bobby accused him of being affiliated with communism:

KENNEDY: If communist unions ever gain a position to exercise influence in the transport lanes of the world, the free world will have suffered a staggering blow.

HOFFA: I am not interested in Beck's politics or his philosophy. I'm interested in the workers.

KENNEDY: Well, do you agree with that?

HOFFA: No, I don't agree with it because the American worker will never put anybody ahead of union. That will disrupt the American system.

KENNEDY: Well, do you know who made that statement?

HOFFA: I don't know, and I don't care. Probably Beck. It sounds like him.

KENNEDY: Mr. James Riddle Hoffa.

HOFFA: I don't believe it.

After insisting that he was impartial to Beck's philosophies and political standing and was solely interested in the workers' welfare, Bobby lightly insinuated that Jimmy may share similar beliefs with his boss. Jimmy flared up, and citizens around the country heard him defend himself: "There is no question about Hoffa, and don't you say that either!" Years down the road, Hoffa would say of Bobby, "He wasn't a good attorney general - in all probability, a worse Senator. I would hate to think what would happen if he became president of the United States. He'd probably have a fascist government."

A picture of Beck (left) clapping

A picture of Bobby and Hoffa at a 1957 hearing

Following the scandal, David Beck resigned under the mounting pressure, and he was later charged with multiple counts of embezzlement, larceny, and income tax evasion. In 1958, after Beck's fall, Jimmy would take his place as residing president of the Teamsters brotherhood, but his presidency would be like nothing he could've imagined. As he once ruefully remarked, "In the old days all you needed was a handshake. Nowadays you need forty lawyers."

Hoffa's turn in the spotlight was far from done, as the Kennedys would latch onto him and make it their mission to bulldoze Jimmy out of the ranks. Three years later, in 1960, when John F. Kennedy began campaigning for the presidential election against Richard Nixon, he called out Jimmy Hoffa in front of the entire nation during the presidential debate in September. Once again enlightening the nation on Jimmy and the Teamsters' alleged crimes, the presidential hopeful mentioned Hoffa while discussing some of the things he wasn't satisfied with in America and wanted to change: "I'm not satisfied when the Soviet Union is turning out twice as many scientists and engineers as we are. I'm not satisfied when many of our teachers are inadequately paid, or when our children go to school part-time shifts. I think we should have an educational system second to none. I'm not satisfied when I see men like Jimmy Hoffa - in charge of the largest union in the United States - still free."

Not surprisingly, the comment infuriated Jimmy, who paraded in front of cameras and played the victim card, criticizing the Kennedys for wanting an innocent, hardworking American in prison. Trapped in the middle of the media frenzy, Jimmy's children recalled their father's concern about the publicity's effects on his family. He would always keep his children in the loop, informing them whenever he could about what stories he heard were about to be publicized. His children spoke of being horrified at the harsh words directed towards their father, much of it consisting of the kind of profanity Jimmy made sure to keep his household free of.

With the Kennedys hot on his trail, Jimmy made sure to stand his ground and attempted to drag their name through the mud. Mostly he focused on Bobby, whom he often mocked and publicly referred to as "Booby." He would go out of his way to humiliate Bobby whenever he could, painting him as a "spoiled, young millionaire" who never had to lift a finger in his life. He was convinced the only reason the Kennedys so urgently wanted him out of the picture was because they couldn't control him.

A year later, when John F. Kennedy became the youngest elected president in American history and appointed his brother Bobby Attorney General, Jimmy's rage was infernal. Disheartened, Jimmy's acquaintances remembered how he would often make the same remark: "Look what money can buy, look what power can buy. Bobby's never tried a case in his life." And when Bobby's first order of business as Attorney General was to form the "Get-Hoffa Squad," acquiring the ammunition of 15 juries nationwide to investigate him, this only intensified Jimmy's undying hatred for the brothers.

Even with the Kennedys now in control of the White House, Jimmy never granted them the respect traditionally associated with the cherished position of power. This was shown on one occasion during a meeting set to take place between Bobby and Jimmy, accompanied by one of his lawyers, Frank Ragano. As expected, Jimmy valued punctuality as a form of respect, and though he was not exactly Bobby's biggest fan, he still made an effort to arrive 15 minutes earlier than the meeting. On the other hand, Bobby ran 45 minutes late, strolling into his office with one of his dogs trotting behind on a leash, coming back from a lengthy walk around the block. Jimmy reputedly sprang up from his seat and charged towards Bobby, clutching him by the throat and throwing him up against the wall. With the President's brother firmly gripped in a stranglehold before stunned authorities interfered, Jimmy managed to berate him for keeping him waiting for some mutt and addressed him with a storm of expletives. After Jimmy was wrested off of him, Bobby simply dusted himself off and exited the room without another word, his growling Saint Bernard trailing behind him. No charges were ever pressed against Jimmy for the incident.

Ragano

What they did charge Hoffa for was a string of crimes that were far more serious than the slap on the wrist that would have ensued from a simple assault charge. Bobby and his committee accused Jimmy of selfishly using Teamsters' pension funds for his own personal gain, accepting illegal bribes and payoffs from trucking companies, and alleged connections with a dangerous racketeer by the name of John Dioguardi. He was indicted in May of 1962, just a year after the Kennedys entered the White House, and with that, it appeared Bobby had stayed true to his word.

Dioguardi, known as Johnny Dio

Jimmy was continuously summoned to hearing after hearing to face seemingly endless questions about pocketing pension funds illegally and using them to pay off mobsters he'd formed alliances with over the years, but once again, throughout the entirety of his hearings, Jimmy denied any involvement or knowledge of his charges. Right before one of his appearances in court, the FBI burst into his office and cuffed him, arresting him on charges of attempting to bribe a lawyer in exchange for classified memos of the Kennedys' committee. Perhaps celebrating a little too early, an overconfident Bobby announced to the nation that justice was served for the notorious Teamster, and if Jimmy still wasn't convicted, he would leap off the top of the Capitol Building. When Jimmy was acquitted on all charges in Nashville after a mistrial resulting from a hung jury, his other lawyer, William E. Bufalino, offered to mail Bobby a parachute.

Bufalino

Realizing his scrappy opponent had reached his position for a reason, Bobby and his committee picked themselves up and proceeded forward with more lawsuits, piling up the charges on Hoffa. The next year, in 1963, Jimmy was indicted once more, this time for jury tampering for the trial in Nashville. In addition to his charges, he was fined another $10,000 (around $78,270 today), but once again, Jimmy slithered his way out of jail time, and for the next several months he would spend most his days trying to elude the many swinging hands of the government eager to snatch him off the streets.

In November of that year, President John F. Kennedy was assassinated, and needless to say, Jimmy wasn't too broken up about the assassination. In fact, he refused to join in the national mourning. One of the best known aspects of Hoffa's multifaceted personality was his temper, and his short fuse shone through on one particular occasion in the wake of the assassination. When an assistant in his office raised the flag outside the building at half-staff to honor the deceased president, Jimmy flew into an explosive, inconsolable rage. The assistant was fired, but not after he was assaulted by his ruddy-faced boss and physically removed from the premises.

The incident concluded with a still-steaming Jimmy storming out to raise the flag himself.

Chapter 4: Shame, Shackles, and a Stab in the Back

"Our rooms were bugged, our phones were tapped, and our lawyer's rooms were broken into and their files stolen. We finally had to hire armed guards with pistols to be able to maintain our records. It was hard to believe we weren't in Russia." – Jimmy Hoffa

When 1964 commenced, Jimmy signed off on a landmark collective contract on the 16th of January. Known as the "National Master Freight Agreement," the document doubled and tripled wages across the country and guaranteed full health benefits for everyone in the Teamsters' union family.

Just four days later, he was convicted for jury tampering in another case in Chattanooga and sentenced to 8 years in prison, and at a second trial later that year, another 5 years was added to his sentence for fraud and conspiracy regarding the Teamster pension fund, comprised of a whopping $1 billion. The light at the end of Jimmy's never-ending tunnel seemed to be dimming fast, the shadow of a dead end visible on the horizon.

51 year old Jimmy and his family were devastated to hear the news of his impending 13 year sentence, but regardless of his conviction and sentencing in 1964, Jimmy and his attorneys would file for multiple appeals for another three years, keeping him free in the meantime. One of their most notable grounds for appeal was that U.S. Marshals had done a little bribing of their own with the jury, palming off alcohol and other gifts to sweeten the deal and thus swaying the verdict in their direction. Astonishingly, the staff that worked in the hotels where jurors rented rooms backed up the defense's strong allegations.

The other charges authorities failed to stick onto Jimmy were no pretty picture either. Among their list of accusations included "shaking down" and harassing company owners for contributions of up to $1 million (almost $8 million today) towards union funds in exchange for "cooperation." Another held him accountable for attempting to surreptitiously tap into the phone lines of his underlings in the Detroit union.

Despite all the media controversy and the gravity of the criminal charges against him, the President of the IBT proclaimed his innocence over and over again, and to the general public, particularly the Teamsters, he was branded an unsung hero. In 1966, while still out on appeal, Jimmy was re-elected as President of the brotherhood by a landslide, and whenever Jimmy and his family walked the streets during what appeared to be his last days of freedom, mobs of supporters rallied around him with picket signs offering words of encouragement. A beaming Jimmy would thank them endlessly, while at the same time blasting the authorities for targeting an honest, guilt-free American. By now, Hoffa was the shepherd of a total of 1.7 million loyal followers, many of whom hung onto his every word, and his already sizable salary of $75,000 ballooned to a clean $100,000, marking him the highest-paid union leader in the United States. He later bragged, "In the ten years I was president of the Teamsters, I had raised the membership from eight hundred thousand to more than 2 million and made it the largest single labor union the world."

However, in 1967, all the hard work done by Jimmy and his attorneys finally collapsed; his appeals were denied, and with that he was to begin his sentence at the high-security Lewisburg Federal Penitentiary in Pennsylvania in March of that year. Bobby Kennedy was overjoyed and couldn't keep himself from shaming Jimmy one last time. He celebrated his victory by issuing a public statement congratulating the lawyers that landed his rival of almost a decade behind bars. A day before Jimmy was scheduled to be shipped off to prison, a confidante revealed that the ostensibly unbreakable man's tough exterior shattered. He was heard pacing around the room, wildly gesturing and almost deliriously repeating: "I'm not going, I'm not going, Joe. I'm not going!"

Ultimately, Hoffa did go, and as he sat caged in a 7 by 10 foot cell, officials from the federal government reportedly stood outside his window, jeering and shouting insults at him. However, Jimmy was adamant to keep control, perhaps also prompted by a bruised ego. Before entering Lewisburg, he productively pushed for an amendment reinforcing his presidency while in captivity and appointed Frank Fitzsimmons as his vice-president. Frank was mostly known as being one of Jimmy's most reliable lackeys, and he even fluffed his boss with menial tasks like pulling out his chair and making coffee runs for him. Many doubted the promotion of the ex-trucker, a rotund man with features reminiscent of a perpetually sad pug, who often exhibited skittishness and uncertainty during his ineloquent public speeches. Still, Jimmy showed complete faith in him, and as the months picked up, his confidence in Frank would prove worthy. Along with running the daily affairs, Frank's public image improved vastly as he won sizable contracts for major national freight agreements and advocated for even more aggressive organizing.

The next year, 1968, would be one that had the nation swimming in turmoil. The United States was in the middle of the messy Vietnam War, packed with its own contentions, and cities were in uproar over the tragic death of Martin Luther King, Jr. In June, about 15 months into Jimmy's sentence, the nation would be rocked by the assassination of Jimmy's main nemesis, Bobby Kennedy. Bobby, who had won a seat in the Senate back in 1964, had been following in his brother's footsteps and sought candidacy for presidency himself. When President Lyndon B. Johnson announced that he would not be running for a second term, the big fish was out the way and things were looking good for him. He was well-received by the public, particularly by minority groups who praised him for his devotion to raise awareness for the Civil Rights Movement, and on June 5, he won the California presidential primary. However, as he was departing from the Ambassador Hotel through the lobby, escorted by star athletes Roosevelt Grier and Rafer Johnson, a Palestinian man named Sirhan Sirhan elbowed through the crowd of well-wishers. Sporting dirty jeans and a plain, light-colored shirt with the first two buttons undone, exposing a tuft of chest hair, the young man with the thick shock of dark curls and a prominent, hooked nose blended in seamlessly. With Bobby's campaign poster ironically wrapped around a 22-caliber revolver and within arm's length, he raised his gun and fired aimlessly. The crowd erupted in chaos amidst the spraying bullets, several of them lodging into Bobby's torso and wounding 5 bystanders. Sirhan Sirhan was apprehended and sentenced to death, and Bobby died the following day. When questioned about his motives, the demented man asserted that Kennedy played an "instrumental" role in the oppression of his people, to the extent that he timed the assassination with the anniversary of the start of the 1967 Six Day War.

When Jimmy got word of his rival's death, he rejoiced in prison. Many predicted that the fervent fire that burned within the imprisoned man, who was now nearing his 60s, would merely be flickering, but Jimmy's reaction suggested the contrary. Life in Lewisburg was by no means ideal or close to the ballpark of actual freedom, but it wasn't the hellhole the majority of the other inmates endured either. In an issue of *Life* magazine published in June of 1971, four years into Jimmy's sentence, an article detailed the union leader's life in prison and divulged that he was living out his shackled days in an "honor dormitory" amongst 79 other inmates, most of them middle-aged and imprisoned for non-violent crimes. He had adequate privacy in his single cell (which would only be bolted shut at night), furnished with a sturdy cot, a desk-and-lamp set, and a small washbasin. Breakfast was served at 6:00 sharp, and by 7:30, he was expected to work in the prison mattress factory. Other than that, he was free to do as he pleased in the evenings and had all weekends off.

To pass the time, Hoffa would read a plethora of whatever books and newspapers he could get his hands on, and occasionally he joined the other inmates for a few hours of television. Even food was considered top-notch to most, with the inmates enjoying fresh meat and milk from the prison farm close by. A thick slab of steak and healthy vegetable medleys were often on the menu. Moreover, his Teamster comrades also ensured he knew he wasn't forgotten; on his 55th birthday, union workers hired a plane to fly over the prison with a banner that read "Free Jimmy Hoffa!"

Even in captivity, Jimmy loathed being idle and working without purpose. Not only did he happily attend to his fellow inmates, who would often ask him for advice, but the prison guards often sought out his help as well. Informally dubbed the business agent for the guards, he would walk them through on how to effectively assemble and organize a union of their own, and they would hold secret meetings, which the prison warden would often break up. Whenever the warden stumbled in on the meetings that persisted, they were rationally reprimanded and disciplined.

Unbeknownst to Jimmy, President Richard Nixon and Frank Fitzsimmons began to work together in cahoots and develop a plan of their own that took advantage of Hoffa being behind bars. Though he was previously denied parole three times, in 1971 Jimmy was visited by his attorneys, and the news they bore stupefied their client: Nixon agreed to grant him a pardon and the freedom he so yearned for if Jimmy was willing to step down from his presidency and keep out of union activities until 1980, the original end date of his sentence. After much consideration, he reluctantly agreed, and thus, two days before Christmas, Hoffa was released from Lewisburg after serving less than 5 years of his 13 year sentence.

Chapter 5: Clinging Onto the Glory Days

"They all know I'm back, very much back, and that I will be the General President again, come hell or high water!"

Though he was anxious to get home to his family, in some ways, Hoffa's release from prison was bittersweet. Accompanying the joys of ambling down unguarded along the Detroit streets, his boots sinking into the thick blanket of December snow, he rushed home to a crowd of Hoffa supporters and the dazzling flashes of the media. News stations broadcasted the tender moment of his arrival, and his daughter Barbara fondly recalled the wide, irrepressible grin on his face upon seeing his family again. Josephine, the rock and love of his life, was front and center waiting by the doorway, and with a brightened face gracefully made-up, an elaborate up-do, and a beautiful crimson Christmas dress for the amazing occasion, his wife pounced on him. She threw her arms around Jimmy, glee-induced tears staining her cheeks.

The family continued their heartwarming reunion indoors, where the Hoffas stuffed themselves with a holiday feast and watched as the young ones ripped off the wrappings of their presents. For the first time, 58 year old Jimmy was introduced to the grandchildren that had been born while he was "away," and he became an instantly adoring grandfather to his two grandsons and granddaughter.

However, while many may have chosen to retire at this point, it was not in Hoffa's DNA. In fact, he remained determined to become President of the IBT again, despite Nixon's demands. It was widely believed that Nixon, who had come to power in 1968, seriously needed to strengthen his chances for the upcoming re-election campaign in 1972. Even as an outspoken Republican, he won over the public by executing what was known as the "Southern Strategy." This entailed an elaborate campaign aggressively highlighting both racial and cultural issues, which won over the hearts of many of the working class both in the North and the South. Nixon decided that if he wanted a second term, he needed to use similar measures, so the president and his aides strove to reconstruct his image with the public once more after facing backlash during his first term, unveiling a side of Nixon that was less anti-labor than previous Republican leaders. The Nixon administration began signing off on deals that would mutually but very privately benefit both them and the unions, and one of his most treasured connections was the Teamsters' acting president, Frank Fitzsimmons.

Fitzsimmons and Nixon

Furthermore, many theorized that Nixon had a soft spot for Fitzsimmons, who wasn't as independent and whose backbone was much easier to mold and manipulate compared to the loud-mouthed Jimmy Hoffa. Fitzsimmons agreed to endorse Nixon for his presidential campaign in 1972, and allegedly, he also agreed to keep the Teamsters from rejoining the American Federation of Labor and Congress of Industrial Organizations (AFL-CIO), the largest federation of unions in the United States. This was supposedly set in place so the Teamsters could perform under-the-table favors for the Republicans. In return, Fitzsimmons needed Nixon's word that Hoffa would never rise to power again. Adding extra sprinkles to the deal, Fitzsimmons also enjoyed a bump in salary, cashing in $125,000 annually.

Of course, when the Watergate scandal broke and the existence of Nixon's White House tapes was revealed, those recordings became evidence. Some of them included lengthy audio of conversations involving or discussing Fitzsimmons, and White House Special Counsel Charles Colson was said to have later written a memo to Nixon boldly proclaiming, "We are with him [Fitzsimmons] all the way, and there will be no concessions with Hoffa."

Regardless of the fact that Nixon was largely to blame for keeping the IBT presidency out of Jimmy's reach, Jimmy never publicly expressed any disdain towards the nation's leader. Instead, he saved his ferocious rage for Fitzsimmons, who was once his most trusted confidante, often slandering him to whoever would listen and depicting him as "a liar" and "a double-crosser." To Jimmy, the betrayal was personal, and it deeply wounded him; after all, this was the man he'd pulled out of a truck to work directly for him, bought him his first suit, and most of all, entrusted his beloved brotherhood of Teamsters to.

Even when Hoffa was awarded $1.7 million from the Teamsters' pension fund all at once in a single payment upon his release, and despite being pestered by his loved ones and friends to retire, Jimmy remained as stubborn as ever. Most who received a lump sum payment nearing $2 million would feel like they won the lottery and would squander away the cash on frivolous items and extravagant parties, or perhaps they'd be halfway across the world on a never-ending vacation. Some might invest it or donate to charities for the much less fortunate. But Jimmy Hoffa had other things in mind with that money.

Along with campaigning for prison reform, Hoffa filed a lawsuit to nullify the restriction barring him from his treasured IBT presidency. Despite everyone around him attempting to persuade him into retirement and to simply let it be, he resisted. He went on to claim that the senior officials of the Nixon administration were conspiring against him and robbing him of his civil rights. Attorney General John Mitchell, Charles Colson, and Fitzsimmons all vigorously denied these accusations till the end of the 1974 court proceedings. Jimmy lost his case, with the court agreeing that Nixon had acted within his right to impose the non-participation restrictions, resulting from Jimmy's own abuse of power as the Teamsters' president.

Colson

Mitchell

Now in his 60s, Jimmy's face was lined with wrinkles creased from stress and age, and the same, slicked back hairstyle he carried throughout his adulthood was streaked with silvery grays. In a rare interview in 1973, Jimmy was asked about restrictions and curfews set to abide by during his early release, one of which included necessitating a special request slip if he wanted to travel out of the Eastern district, but it appeared he had no qualms about the limitations of his new freedom. His only concern revolved around obtaining the power he felt was unjustly taken from his grasp. He was often heard crying in anguish, "Get the rats off the ship!" The fact that there was nothing he could do about it was destroying him inside.

As Hoffa grew older, he only became brasher, but at the same time, the Nixon administration and his former underling Fitzsimmons weren't the only ones who wanted him off the roster for good. Like many other unions, the Teamsters were still puppeteered by nefarious, turf-protective mobsters, and they weren't happy with Jimmy's relentless drive to rise back to the top. Even his son, James Phillip, who was then in his mid-30s, worried tirelessly over his father's safety and implored him to be extra careful when he was out and about on his own. To this, Jimmy brushed his son off: "I don't need no bodyguards. Who'd wanna kill me?"

On the 30th of July in 1975, Jimmy slipped into a blue shirt, a crisp pair of jeans, and squirmed into a pair of clean white socks. Kissing his wife on the cheek goodbye, he snatched up his keys and left their home in Lake Orion. He drove his 1974 Pontiac Grand Ville to 6676 Telegraph Road. Never a minute late to his meetings, at 2:00 p.m. sharp, he stopped at the parking lot of a local restaurant in the Bloomfield Township area called the Machus Red Fox Restaurant. In Jimmy's diary entry, he'd written that he was to have a meeting with two powerful men with supposed mob connections that ran deep: Anthony Giacalone, one of the most prominent figures of the Detroit underworld, and Anthony Provenzano, a Teamsters union leader from New Jersey who was one of Jimmy's closest acquaintances.

Giacalone

Provenzano

A picture of the restaurant

When no one showed up after half an hour, an agitated Jimmy exited his car and squeezed into an empty phone booth. He rang home and spoke with his wife, expressing his frustrations of their no-show. After informing her that he'd wait around for a few more minutes, he hung up. That was the last time Josephine ever heard her husband's rough, gravelly voice.

Jimmy's family reported him missing when he failed to return home that evening. Meanwhile, his car sat unlocked and unscathed in the parking lot, with no tangible clue as to his whereabouts. A truck driver placed Jimmy in a maroon vehicle with an unknown passenger, and he claimed there was a long, rifle-like object sandwiched between them. However, when it came to the courtroom, both Giacalone and Provenzano declined that a meeting was even supposed to take place, and they provided airtight alibis. Eventually, all the witnesses pleaded the Fifth Amendment and retracted their statements, and with no concrete evidence to satisfactorily tie anyone to Hoffa's bizarre disappearance, he was declared legally dead 7 years later in 1982.

In the wake of his disappearance, Jimmy's family was distraught, especially his wife, who never reverted to the old Josephine her family once knew. *People* magazine described the scene in the Hoffa household a few weeks after Jimmy's disappearance, during which his family continued to hold out hope: "Inside the Jimmy Hoffa family kept a stoic vigil. In the oak-paneled, blue-carpeted living room Barbara Hoffa Crancer sat by an unlisted telephone that had been hooked into a cassette recorder. A handwritten reminder, 'Don't stay on too long!', was Scotch-taped to a lamp. Nearby her brother, James, fielded incoming calls on another phone. In the kitchen their dazed mother, Josephine Hoffa, and a friend washed dishes after a chicken tetrazzini dinner. Nearly a week had passed since husband and father Jimmy, the feisty, erstwhile boss of the International Brotherhood of Teamsters, had vanished. 'My father always said the two worst things were kidnapping little kids for money and dope-pushing,' said Barbara. 'He would think it was disgusting to take a man away from his family.'"

Hoffa's heartbroken wife died 5 years later after suffering a mild stroke, never finding out what really happened to husband, and in the decades since, the mysterious disappearance of Jimmy Hoffa is still a question that all but invites people to attempt to decipher.

Chapter 6: Theories

"I heard you paint houses." - Jimmy Hoffa to Frank Sheeran

People love a classic "whodunnit" mystery, and over the years, some ridiculous theories have surfaced surrounding the case, many of them justifying a good bout of head-scratching. One of these theories belonged to Tom Dawson, a retired car salesman, who began circulating his claims two years after Jimmy went missing. A citizen of Atlanta, Georgia, over 722 miles and a good 11-hour drive away, he swore he watched aliens drag Jimmy aboard a 50-foot spacecraft. The aliens – depicted as 7 petite, hairless creatures with sharp noses and ears – communicated in freakishly shrill gibberish. Dawson reported that he'd heard three repeated cries of "I am Jimmy Hoffa!" before he blacked out. During the abduction, Dawson and Jimmy were supposedly probed by aliens in an "invasive medical exam" before the witness was released. Though Dawson was apparently beamed back to Earth unharmed, Jimmy was never heard from again. Many attributed Dawson's "out of this world" tale to the Steven Spielberg movie that was released the same year: *Close Encounters of the Third Kind.*

20 years later, in 1995, another unidentified man raised more eyebrows when he professed that Hoffa visited him in an "ESP (Extrasensory Perception) dream." The unlikely psychic, an avid fan devoted to the famous science fiction TV hit *The X-Files*, told authorities that Jimmy himself claimed to be buried in a house at the Waterford Township in Michigan, close to Detroit. The man urged the FBI to hurry, as there was a "terrible smell," presumably of Jimmy's decomposing body, wafting from the alleged burial site. Desperate officials followed up on the lead for months. Empty fields were swept through multiple times, and a suspicious barn was even torn down. As many expected, their search turned up empty.

A few hopefuls attempted to start rumors that followed legends such as Tupac Shakur, Elvis Presley, and more recently, Michael Jackson: what if Jimmy Hoffa was still alive? Another Teamster by the name of Rolland McMaster would sprout a fascinating, scandalous theory often heard only in the impeccably dramatic writing of soap operas. It was his belief that Jimmy had simply upped and left Josephine to be with his secret lover, a "black go-go dancer." Apparently the man had abandoned his old family to raise his two illegitimate young children in South America. This story was quickly stowed away by the multitudes who believed Jimmy's only other mistress was his work. However, a more sinister reason why the FBI doubted McMaster's story was because the man was once a suspect himself, and a close accomplice had apparently come forward with the gun used to off Jimmy.

McMaster

Naturally, when an unsolved mystery persists for as long as Jimmy's disappearance has, there are a few who have more morbid takes on the situation. Among the goldmine of files containing information on the case that were disclosed to the public in 2011, papers detailed the investigation of a meat-packing plant by a man named Allen Dorfman. Dorfman was another Teamsters official and a notable figure in the Chicago criminal underworld who would himself be gunned down in 1983. Mobsters were said to have gotten rid of him to prevent him from snitching to authorities in order to weasel himself out of a 55-year sentence on charges of fraud and bribery. He was also said to have been linked to Jimmy's abrupt departure and was strongly suspected by authorities to have fed Jimmy's remains through his fat-rendering processor, but Dorfman's plant dubiously burned down in an unexplained fire, apparently destroying all evidence. Another source later told authorities that Anthony Provenzano "garroted" Jimmy before running his lifeless torso through a wood chipper.

Dorfman

Then, there was Chuckie O'Brien, Jimmy's foster son and one of the men who would take the Fifth Amendment in the 1974 hearings pertaining to Jimmy's case. He was accused of driving the maroon vehicle the truck driver witness had seen him in, a car that belonged to the son of Anthony Giacalone. DNA evidence was reportedly uncovered in the backseat implicating Jimmy's presence in the car, but until the day he died, O'Brien insisted that he would never have betrayed the man who'd so selflessly taken him under his wing. In an interview with journalist Morley Safer in an episode of *60 Minutes*, the accused denounced Agent James Esposito, who'd written up the affidavit placing O'Brien as one of the main participants in Jimmy's abduction, as a "liar." However, when Jimmy's son confronted O'Brien and demanded to know what had happened to his father and whether or not he was involved, O'Brien's response was to "run out of the room" without saying another word.

O'Brien

Over the decades, some people suddenly decided to step forward after years of silence, clicking off their mute buttons to spread word that they were the ones responsible for the missing Teamsters leader. It was apparent these people wanted credit for the legendary disappearance, but many of them were quickly determined to be unreliable sources grabbing blindly at an extra 15 minutes of fame.

One of these individuals was a late mobster named Phillip Moscato, whose story was told through Dan Moldea, an investigative reporter. Moldea promised he wouldn't unleash Moscato's story and "sell him out" until after the mobster's passing, and with that, Moscato pointed the finger at a known enforcer named Salvatore Briguglio, one of Provenzano's henchmen. Though Briguglio was fingered as the culprit who'd pulled the trigger, Moscato claimed to have played an integral role in the shady scheme. Along with driver Ralph Picardo, the three supposedly crammed Jimmy's corpse into a 55-gallon drum and buried him. The drum was believed to be entombed under a Michigan farm, but Moscato refused to reveal the actual location, other than that the barrel was caked under toxic soil in New Jersey. Another man claiming to be one of Hoffa's murderers was Richard Kuklinski, a supposed mob contract killer, who confessed on his deathbed to stabbing Jimmy on the side of the head with a hunting dagger. He then proceeded to drive Hoffa's body to a faraway scrap metal yard.

Briguglio

Obviously the case has not yet been solved, but perhaps one of the most riveting and plausible theories came from yet another late mobster, Frank "The Irishman" Sheeran. In an episode entitled *"Who Killed Jimmy Hoffa?"* on the PBS show *History Detectives,* Sheeran's biographer Charles Brandt discussed Sheeran's past and potential connection to Hoffa. Incidentally, the title of the biography, *I Heard You Paint Houses*, were the first words Jimmy greeted Sheeran with. This seemingly innocent line served a hidden meaning as lingo for being a contract killer, and the paint hinted at in the phrase referred to blood splatter that would ensue from a shooting.

Sheeran

Sheeran was characterized as a man who'd begun life with an average, almost vanilla lifestyle whose criminal record was a clean slate until World War II. During the war, he underwent laborious training in combat that spanned over 400 days when most averaged 80, and he emerged as a prolific killer. After the war, he began contract killing for a ruthless but venerated mobster by the name of Russell Bufalino, a distant relative of one of Jimmy's attorneys, William Bufalino. It was reportedly through Russell that Sheeran crossed paths with Jimmy, at a time when the union leader was facing problems with uncooperative factions in both Philadelphia and Detroit. Sheeran was christened the Teamster Organizer for Detroit, and he thus began following Jimmy around as his "personal hit man."

Russell Bufalino

Sheeran repeatedly emphasized that he loved Jimmy and his entire family, maintaining in his own words, "There was a lot of shit...it never should have happened." According to the self-described hit man, instead of Provenzano or Giacalone, it was him who'd pulled up next to Jimmy outside the phone booth shortly after he'd just rung Josephine. Sheeran explained that there was a change in plans, and that the meeting place had been altered to an unmarked house, where Russell Bufalino would be there to mediate. To Jimmy, who was well-versed with Provenzano's unpredictable and volatile temper, he assumed that Russell's presence would be an advantage on his part; since he and the mob boss had long been amicable acquaintances up to this point, he believed the quiet, outwardly reserved Russell would help keep the peace. Jimmy and Provenzano's last meeting had ended violently, with both men stubborn as mules and equipped with clashing, but similarly fickle anger issues. Provenzano was said to have even gone so far as to threaten to kidnap Jimmy's granddaughter.

According to Sheeran's version, the minute Hoffa set foot into the building, a peculiar feeling had to have been stewing in his gut. All the tell-tale signs of a meeting - the distant sound of whispered Italian lingering in the air, the platters of piping-hot food displayed across the tables, the scuffing of shuffling feet and chairs squeaking across the floorboards –were clearly absent. Jimmy instantly pieced together the plan in his mind and did a quick 180, but just as he edged past Sheeran through the doorway, his old friend of 20 some years shot him twice in the back of the head execution style, the deafening shots reverberating through the eerily vacant house. Sheeran confided in Brandt that he'd never been able to live down killing his friend, but if he hadn't complied with Russell's orders, his life would have been on the line and Hoffa would have still been "just as dead." He implied that in a way, he'd saved Jimmy from what would have been a much more horrifying fate.

Sheeran's account has led people to wonder why Russell Bufalino wanted Hoffa out of the way so badly. In 1941, after Jimmy had hired "mafia goons" to keep rival mobs out of his territory, he'd entered an unbreakable pact with the mob. To give a better picture as to just how great Jimmy's influence was in the trucking industry, it was said that at his peak, he virtually controlled everything on wheels. This included gas, oil, steel, and all the goods in grocery and department stores. The mobsters supposedly acted as the supportive wind pumping beneath his wings and elevating him to the top, but in exchange, the mob required payoffs, "sweetheart contracts," and union jobs with fat, overly generous paychecks.

Though Jimmy would deny it until the day he vanished, the Teamsters' $1 billion pension funds was like the mobsters' private slush fund. These illegal transactions allegedly helped build a swanky empire of mobster-owned hotels and casinos in Las Vegas. When asked about this, Hoffa demurred, saying, "Sure, we loaned money to build hotels and casinos in Las Vegas. So what? Las Vegas borrowers were good customers." However, under his leadership, the Teamsters' funds were making immense loans of $1-10 million to gambling and resort establishments along the Las Vegas strip.

After 1967, the year Jimmy was sent to prison, the loans to these establishments doubled, and at times, tripled in size, under the man who'd betrayed Jimmy: Frank Fitzsimmons. It was believed that the mobsters began fearing that Jimmy, who towards the end of his life was fighting hard to regain his old presidency, would impart their criminal activities to authorities. They wanted to keep Fitzsimmons, a spineless yes-man in power, and to Russell Bufalino, getting rid of Jimmy was simply business.

Authorities investigated the validity of Sheeran's claims by following up on another one of his claimed kills: the infamous gangster Joseph "Crazy Joe" Gallo, who was gunned down in a Manhattan restaurant on April 7, 1972 by multiple unidentified shooters. Though authorities were never able to close the case and didn't release any names, a witness who requested to remain anonymous came forward. Just 19 at the time, the witness recalled sitting next to Gallo's table facing Mulberry Street in Little Italy when a tall, red-haired man in a corduroy jacket strolled in and stopped next to Gallo and his friends. Within seconds, an explosive bang sounded, and a lifeless Gallo was slumped over in his seat. As she leafed through photographs of different suspects, she selected Frank Sheeran, and though she had never heard of the man before, she was positive he was the same man who'd killed Gallo.

Gallo

Sheeran's biographer would later back up his client's story by asserting that every time he'd inquire into the details to Jimmy's disappearance, the retelling would be told in the exact same way. However, some are still skeptical, chalking up Sheeran's story to yet another last attempt at fame on his deathbed. For one thing, his account of Gallo's murder is quite different than other accounts, including accounts told by members of the Colombo crime family that allegedly ordered the hit. Additionally, when authorities searched the house mentioned in Sheeran's story, blood was found on the floorboards, but it wasn't Hoffa's.

The engrossing topic of Jimmy Hoffa and the man behind the porous mystery has made its way into dozens of books, documentaries, and even a Danny DeVito film simply entitled *Hoffa*. Hoffa's mysterious case still occasionally springs up in the news, and authorities continue to search here and there for new clues or even remains. The amount of money the federal government has spent over the years excavating properties based on flimsy leads is staggering, and in 2006 alone, a single search in Michigan lasted two weeks and cost about $250,000.

Through it all, Little Jimmy, now better known to the world as James Phillip Hoffa, is continuing his father's legacy. He's an accomplished attorney and the General President of the International Brotherhood of Teamsters, currently serving his fifth consecutive term. Today, the IBT is home to around 1.4 million unionized workers and another 500,000 retirees spread across the United States.

To Jimmy Hoffa's sea of rivals, the man's unsolvable disappearance brought nothing but convenience. To the famed Strawberry Boys and his army of supporters and confidantes, the loss of their comrade was a downright shame, but to many, it was a completely expected end. To Jimmy's family – Josephine, now long gone, and Jimmy's children, now grandparents themselves – it is a gaping crevice that can never be filled, and they are painfully aware that they may never see closure in their lifetime.

As for the rest of the world, many will continue to be interested if not nosy bystanders, and they will continue to sift through all the different stories and theories.

Online Resources

Other titles about 20th century history by Charles River Editors

Other titles about Jimmy Hoffa on Amazon

Bibliography

Ashenfelter, David. "Jimmy Hoffa Flashback, 2004: Was Hoffa Killed inside Northwest Detroit Home?" Detroit Free Press. Gannett Company, 27 Sept. 2012. Web. 19 Oct. 2015.

Thomas, Tiffany. "4 Jimmy Hoffa Conspiracy Theories That Persist To This Day, 40 Years After His Disappearance." Bustle. Bustle.com, 30 July 2014. Web. 19 Oct. 2015.

Jimmy Hoffa: The Man Behind the Mystery. Dir. Max J. Miller. A&E Television Networks, 2000. Film.

Kalikow, Lisa, dir. "Who Killed Jimmy Hoffa?" History Detectives. Detroit, Michigan, 6 Oct. 2014. Television.

Landsburg, Alan, prod. "Jimmy Hoffa." In Search Of... Leonard Nimoy. 20 Nov. 1980. Television.

Russell, Thaddeus. Out Of The Jungle: Jimmy Hoffa And The Remaking Of (Labor In Crisis). Temple UP, 2003. Print.

"1964: Hoffa Faces Eight Years behind Bars." BBC. MMVII, 12 Mar. 1964. Web. 20 Oct. 2015.

"'Vendetta' Recalls The Ruthless Rivalry Between Bobby Kennedy, Jimmy Hoffa." NPR. NPR, 6 July 2015. Web. 21 Oct. 2015.

Taylor, Troy. "THE MISSING TEAMSTER What Happened to Union Leader Jimmy Hoffa?" Dead Men Do Tell Tales. Troy Taylor Copyright, 8 Sept. 2004. Web. 21 Oct. 2015.

"Robert Holmes 1913-2006." International Metropolis. Tempera & Wordpress, 21 Feb. 2006. Web. 21 Oct. 2015.

"Worker Receives Ten Hilarious Formal Complaints in Six Months."Sabotage Times. Sabotage, 25 Dec. 2013. Web. 21 Oct. 2015.

Marzulli, John. "EXCLUSIVE: New Evidence Emerges on Jimmy Hoffa's Possible Fate, Suggests Feds Were on Right Track Searching N.J. Dump."Daily News. NYDailyNews.com, 30 July 2015. Web. 21 Oct. 2015.

Greengard, Samuel. "Playing It Safe: A Look at Workplace Safety During the Roaring '20s and Now." Workforce. Saba, 4 Jan. 2012. Web. 22 Oct. 2015.

Zennie, Michael. "Jimmy Hoffa's Body Was Run through a WOOD CHIPPER, and That His Remains Will Never Be Found, Says Source." Daily Mail Online. Associated Newspapers Ltd, 20 June 2013. Web. 22 Oct. 2015.

Turk, John. "Mob Underboss Says Jimmy Hoffa Was "buried Alive" at Dig Site in Oakland Township." Oakland Press News. The Oakland Press, 17 June 2013. Web. 23 Oct. 2015.

Lebergott, Stanley. "The Concise Encyclopedia of Economics: Wages and Working Conditions." Library of Economics and Liberty. Liberty Fund, Inc., 29 Mar. 2002. Web. 23 Oct. 2015.

Witheridge, Annette. "My Father Was the Mafia Hitman Who Killed Jimmy Hoffa." MailOnline. Associated Newspapers Ltd, 20 Mar. 2011. Web. 23 Oct. 2015.

Wisely, John. "40 Years Later, Jimmy Hoffa Mystery Endures." USA Today. Gannett Company, 30 July 2015. Web. 23 Oct. 2015.

Jones, Thom L. "The Disappearance of Jimmy Hoffa." Gangsters Inc. Ning Mode, 17 Nov. 2010. Web. 23 Oct. 2015.

Leach, Michelle. "10 Theories on Jimmy Hoffa's Final Fate."Listosaur.Com. Listosaur.Com, 14 Feb. 2013. Web. 23 Oct. 2015.

"Top Guy at Lewisburg." Life Magazine 18 June 1971: 73. Print.

Printed in Great Britain
by Amazon